Heavenly Waves

Angel Yager

BookLeaf Publishing

Presentation by *BookLeaf Publishing*

Web: www.bookleafpub.com

E-mail: info@bookleafpub.com

ISBN: 9789357440370

First edition 2023

DEDICATION

I dedicate this book to my sons Jody Justice Hayes and Josiah D'Angelo Hayes, who make me so proud, everyday of our lives. I love you guys!!

ACKNOWLEDGEMENT

I'm where I'm at through God, who makes all things possible!

PREFACE

This book of poetry is about the hardships in life and how God helps me through it all. Life isn't easy but a positive mindset and a lot of FAITH, goes a long way.

"When we get to Heaven"

Until I get to heaven, I simply can't wait.
I'll get to meet Jesus, at those Pearly Gates.
All worries will be lifted off our shoulders like weight.
And i anticipate, feeling love WITHOUT hate.
When we get to Heaven, we'll feel no more pain.
We won't have to struggle or feel any strain.
nobody's homeless, or left cold in the rain.
And everyone is beautiful, yet no one is vain.
When we get to Heaven, we'll have no more debt.
We will not feel ashamed or have any regrets.
No one will cry, and nobody's upset.
Everyone's laughing with nothing to fret.
When we get to Heaven, there won't be guns.
Nobody's killing each other for drugs.
The only addiction you'll have, is to "LOVE".
Addicted to loving one another, and hugs.
When I get to Heaven, they'll be a smile on my face.
Cuz no one will be judged by religion or race.
There won't be any bullying, or anyone disgraced.
And everyone's welcomed, that the Lord calls to his place.
When we get to Heaven, they'll be no more sorrow.
You won't have to fear, who's dying tomorrow.
Time will not matter, it's a no longer borrowed.
Each day will be beautiful, and so will tomorrow.
When we get to Heaven, we'll have no more fear.
We won't have the devil, to whisper lies in our ear.
There won't be temptation of sin while we're here.
And everyone's happy and shedding no tears.
When we get to heaven, it'll be a glorious sight.

With streets made of gold and souls that glow bright.
Everything Glitters and glistens so right.
And there's beautiful flowers that are such a delight.
When we get to heaven, we will know we are home.
No one will know depression, or feeling alone.
Everyone's happy and joyous to roam.
Communicating in Harmony, and you won't need a phone.
When we get to Heaven, our souls will glow.
Our gowns will be white and will hang down low.
But they will not be heavy, we'll be weightless you know.
Floating about, leaving burdens below.
When we get to Heaven, we'll be home at last.
And nobody's judged by the sins of their past.
All will be forgiven, as soon as they ask.
And everyone's honest, no one wears a mask.
When we get to Heaven, our souls will be free.
Our sins will be lifted off of you and me.
We'll be light as a feather, and bright as can be.
And colors so beautiful, only Heaven can see.
So i simply can't wait, to be bonded so strong.
Where everyone is equal and we all get along.
We'll finally be HOME, after waiting so long.
Cuz when we get to Heaven, we'll be where we BELONG.

"Step into the light"

I opened my eyes and stepped into the light.
I saw what was wrong so i made it right.
I was blinded for years without any sight.
But i opened my eyes to a future so bright.
I realized my destiny is in my own hands.
And no other person can ruin my plans.
Without my consent, they have no ground to stand.
Won't make me nor break me, no woman nor man.
Your happiness depends on the actions YOU take.
You make your own fate with the choices you make.
You can not pass blame for your own mistakes.
You live and you learn from each heartache.
So i made it RIGHT, where i went WRONG.
And i found in life where i belong.
I've made mistake as i've come along.
I've learned from them which made me strong.
I once was BLIND, but now i see.
My happiness depends on only ME.
I opened my eyes to my DESTINY.
And my future is WHATEVER i make it to be!

"Through the eyes of a Grieving mother"

"Through the eyes of a grieving mother"
(Dedicated to anyone who ever lost a child)

How can I cope, when I can't comprehend,
that my child is gone and I can't see them again?
How can I heal when I can't even pretend,
to care about life, or living again?
How can I get over the anger inside,
when my child's no longer standing right by my side?
I cannot feel happy, no matter how hard I've tried.
So I've cried and I've cried, and feel dead now inside.
How can I force myself to get out of bed,
When I was hoping the Lord would strike me dead?
That way I'd be with my child instead,
of living without them, like any parent would dread.
These are just some, of the things I will feel.
A numbness inside, that prohibits me to heal.
I'll never get over what doesn't seem real.
And words can't express this pain that I feel.
Nothing will matter when your child is gone.
Please take me now to the heavens Beyond.
Where my child and I can swim free, in the pond,
of Purity and happiness and continue our bond.
I live for the day to go home in the sky.
To live up in heaven, my child and I.
to be hand-in-hand, again this is why,

I continue to live, I continue to try.
How do I cope with being so stressed,
when my heart is being ripped, right out of my chest?
This is my child, I fed from my breast.
And I gave them my all, and I gave them my best.
Without them I'm lost, no reason to live.
And it's easy to blame God,as our perogative.
But God understands and even forgives,
and one day the answer will make sense, that HE gives.
How can I smile when I feel guilty inside?
Guilty to live life without my kid by my side.
How can I let myself, find happiness or Pride?
when punishing myself , is what's really on my mind.
I say to my child. "watch over me from up above."
"Will YOU think, if i'm happy, I might have lost love?
"How do I move on without your kisses and hugs?
I will mourn you forever and ever, my love!
but I know that it hurts you, to see mommy sad.
You would want me to smile and to always feel glad.
But life without you, is nothing but bad.
Cuz you were my child, the strongest bond that I've had.
Please help your mom, I'm at the end of my rope.
and I'm needing guidance, your strength and some
hope.
I'll NEVER get over you, but please help me to cope.
And send me some healing, for this heart that is broke.
I know that you're here with me, my child of mine.
Your spirit is strong, please send me a sign.
I just want to know that you're happy,doing fine.
And we still are together till the end of time.
Without You I'm weak, please help me be strong.
Please help your mother to get along.

I know that beside you, is where I belong.
So show me your guidance, when I am wrong.
I live for the day, you'll be back in my arms.
And Heaven is that place, of beautiful charms.
Where nothing can hurt you, no worries of harm.
And we can rest easy, no need for alarm.
I want you to know, Mommy did all that she can,
To protect you in life, under my guiding hands.
I hope that you know and understand,
That the love of a mother, for her child, is GRAND.
So walk with me now, and guide your mother tonight.
Protect me and Wrap Me In Your Arms so tight.
And when it is time to go toward that light.
Yake me by the hand, and guide me RIGHT."
Cause without my Faith, my healing couldn't begin.
Only through God will we meet up again.
I must walk with Jesus, and repent all my sins.
Then my questions can be answered when I see u
again....

"Ugly"

I never realized how ugly I was.
Was i walking around all day with a buzz?
I didn't even see how TOXIC I was.
Cuz ugly is, as ugly does.
I'm not that person. I'm not the same.
I look back now and feel ashamed.
My actions were ugly, and I was to blame.
And I didn't have Jesus to clear my name.
I was so bad, and thought vengeance was mine.
Spiteful and evil and thought that was fine.
I should've known then that I was ugly inside.
And ugly inside, means ugly outside.
Lord forgive me, I'm still not my best.
But I'm learning from you how to love all the rest.
I forgive all my enemies and wish them the best.
And realize with Jesus, I am so blessed.
Help me Lord, to see the beauty within.
To see someone do wrong, and to not judge their sin.
Their sin is no bigger than the sin that i'm in.
Cuz sin is sin, and we're all guilty within.
I wish I knew then, what i know now.
Because I lost a few friends, and lost a few pals.
But I WASN'T THEN, who I am NOW.
CUZ JESUS SAVED ME, and that is how.
I hope everyone sees we can all change our ways.
But WITHOUT KNOWING GOD, the same we shall stay.
If you wanna do better, just kneel down and pray.
And ask Jesus to walk with you for the rest of your days.

"Slipping away"

By ANGEL YAGER

I need your forgiveness Lord, I pray that you can.
I've been slipping away from you, since I lost my man.
I can't do it without you, I'm needing your hand,
To pick me back up, so again I can Stand.
I was doing so good, following your rules.
But lately been slipping and acting a fool.
I'm off of the path, I need to be schooled,
And need to be scolded, when losing my cool.
My mind's in the gutter, my head's in the clouds.
I've been on some trash and I'm not feeling proud.
I know what there is, and what isn't allowed.
I'm needing your guidance, and I'll scream it out loud.
I don't deserve your forgiveness, I don't deserve YOU.
I deserve what I get for the things that I do.
I've been acting up lately, for the past month or two.
I need my head in the book and my mind on YOU.
So forgive me please, for the things that I've said.
The words that I've spewed, and the thoughts in my head.
Forgive me for losing my temper instead,

of handing it to you, to put it to bed.
Forgive me for wandering and losing my way.
For roaming around and running astray.
Forgive me for forgetting to kneel down and pray.
I should have done better, at the end of the day.
I need to focus on YOU, and work on myself.
I can't lead others to you Lord, if I don't fix myself.
So I'll put all my worries away on a self,
And put my faith in you GOD, and NOBODY else.

"My beautiful mother"

The last couple of weeks, of you in that bed,
I keep seeing them over and over again.
So tiny and weak and frail, as we'd dread.
These traumatizing moments are stuck in my head.
And these tears that i shed, are not even fair.
My mom should be here, but instead she's up there.
Did you feel me in the hospital, combing your hair,
And putting your lotion on you, with care?
Nothing compares to a mother's love.
You loved all of us kids, more than we could dream of.
And now you are guiding us all from above.
You're free to fly high, as free as the dove.
And with love, we were beside you holding your hand.
We tried to hold on, when you couldn't stand.
We didn't want to let go, held on as long as we can,
But it was YOUR TIME to go, it was GOD'S plan.
God held out his hand and took you away.
I'm in shock and devastated, still today.
But SO HAPPY for YOU, you're in HEAVEN to stay.
And we WILL get to see you, again ONE day!!

"Give it to Jesus"

"Give it to Jesus, cause he's the one that frees us."
He frees us from our past, and every last mistake.
Frees us from our paths, and every road we take.
Frees us from our feelings, and heals our hearts that break.
And frees us from addiction, now sober we will wake.
He frees us from our habits, the ones we'd like to quit.
And frees us from the chains of love we often find unfit.
He frees us from the kind of spouse that never can commit.
And breaks us free of anyone, who often likes to hit.
Jesus, always frees us, from pain that we endure.
And frees us once again, when we keep running back for more.
He frees us from anxiety, when we're stressed down to the core.
And let's us break away, and flee, so freely out the door.
"SO GIVE IT ALL TO JESUS, CUZ HE'S THE ONE THAT FREES US.
AND IF WE DO, WE'LL BE LIKE NEW, SO GIVE IT ALL TO JESUS....."
He frees us from OURSELVES, from choices we have made.
And frees us from the heaviness, our burdens they have weighed.
He frees us from our demons, who have come back out to play.
And even breaks us free from fear, when all we do is pray.
Jesus always frees us, but first we must believe.
Then we ask, work toward the task, and then we may recieve.
If Jesus doesn't free us yet, please don't be deceived.

It just might be, he'll set us free, but first we have to grieve.
So Jesus can you free us, from depression that we feel?
Free us please, and let it ease, the grief is so unreal.
Free us from the loneliness, and pain that doesn't heal.
I believe that we must grieve, to set free the pain we feel.
"SO GIVE IT ALL TO JESUS, CUZ HE'S THE ONE THAT FREES US.
AND IF WE DO, WE'LL BE LIKE NEW, SO GIVE IT ALL TO JESUS.. GIVE IT ALL TO JESUS!!!"

"How do we know"

How do we know what's real and what's fake?
How do we know which will make our heart ache?
How do we know which path to choose?
With which one we'll win and which one we'll lose.
How do we know which road to travel?
Which will be smooth and which will be gravel.
So I stand at an intersection lost and confused,
Cuz only God will know which road I shall choose.

"So tired"

I'm tired of pain, tired of aches.
Tired of funerals, tired of wakes.
Tired of going through so many heartaches.
I feel like I've taken, all I can take.
But under this pressure I'm not going to break.
So never mistake, because my faith will NOT shake.
I'm not going to flake, on what I believe.
Not through my struggles, and not when I grieve.
Not when I'm angry or when I'm deceived.
I'll always praise God and I'll always believe.
I'll always achieve, with God at my side.
Even down on my luck with a broken down ride.
I'll never blame God no matter how hard I've cried.
I know there's a reason for all who have died.
But I wish I knew why, wish I knew well.
I wish I had answers for all I could tell.
But I still kept my faith, no matter how hard I fell.
Believe that our God would pull us out of this hell.
All will be well, when Jesus comes back.
Believe it or not, but it's all on track.
He's coming to take all the good ones back.
And the rest will be left, so watch how you act.
Get it together, because the time is near.
You might laugh now, but later you'll hear.

The sound of the trumpets in everyone's ear.
So repent for your sins now, so you won't be in fear.
Gather your peers, get everyone here.
Jesus is coming and we'll all be in tears.
We have to get ready and we've known it for years.
And everyone coming will celebrate with cheers.

"Such a sinner"

I'm such a sinner, how could it be,
that God sent his son to rescue me?
Nobody's perfect, I'm flawed as can be,
but Jesus still decided, to die for me.
I can't even imagine the type of love,
that's descending from Heaven, and lives up above.
If I do not repent, when push comes to shove,
I will not be going there, or even thought of.
And if I don't change, I'll be here on my own.
I can't expect God then, to throw me a bone.
He gave me an invitation to come live in his home,
But if I don't seek forgiveness, I'll be left here to roam.
When the sky opens up, and Jesus appears,
all of us laughing, will now be in tears.
All of us sinners are now facing our fears,
despite all the warnings we've heard for years.
When Jesus comes back and descends from the sky,
we'll drop down to our knees and begin to cry.
We'll watch as the worthy disappear in the sky.
And we'll plead and beg Jesus, for another try.
We'll be sorry we waited, until it's too late.
Cuz when the Rapture comes, it seals Our Fate.
God loves us all, but don't hesitate,
Repent your sins now, without the debate.
Because those left behind, that didn't believe,

will wish they had faith, when they fall to their knees.
Satan will make sure that you suffer and grieve,
An eternal damnation, you never can leave.
I hope this sinks in, a message received.
So repent for your sins, I'm begging you please!

"Demons"

When Satan sends DEMONS to get in my way,
I duck and Dodge them EVERYDAY.
he brings them in to knock me down,
But I've got ANGELS all around.
I've got JESUS at my side,
He lifts me up, I'm filled with pride.
When Satan comes for his attack,
Take a seat, GOD'S got my back.
your HARSHEST words I will not stress.
"Not TODAY Satan", you tried your best.
Keep your demons Under Wraps.
Don't send them here to try no crap.
I've got FAITH, that's got my back.
Your BEST attempt won't make me crack.
So take a seat, DEMONS and watch me PRAY,
And watch God bless me, EVERY WAY!

"Take it all"

Take my worries, take my pain.
Wash my sorrows in the rain.
Take my problems from my hand.
Carry me Lord, through the sand.
Pick me up when I am down.
Lift my spirits off the ground.
Give me courage, give me pride.
Fill me up with love, inside.
I take my problems, I lift them up.
Give them to YOU GOD, you fill my cup.
It's runneth over, from all your love.
You bless me here, from up above.
I am NOTHING, without YOU.
I'd be so empty, I'd be so blue.
I'd be of this world, I'd still be lost.
Be filled with sins, and pay the cost.
I'd be greedy, jealous, and vain.
Ungrateful and hateful, and always complain.
Sad and mad and filled with fear.
Lustful and distrustful of anyone near.
I thank you Lord that you forgive.
Gave YOU my heart, you gave me reason to live.
You allowed me to change and forgive all my sins.
But change only occurred, because I let YOU in.
So thank you Lord, I'm now REVIVED.
Filled with your love, I NOW feel ALIVE!!

"Break me, to make me"

Demons, back up.
I'm tired of hurting from all the bad luck.
But I refuse to give up...
I remain, constantly in pain, and feeling so stuck.
Seeing so many doctors I don't know what to do.
My life is consumed in these rooms without views.
I'm tired of bad news.
Got me so stressed and depressed, with the Blues.
This is not what I choose, not what I chose.
Everytime I get news another problem arose.
You think I get used to the highs and the lows.
but I'm tired of waking and taking these blows.
God only knows, I'm needing a break.
So many disorders it must be a mistake.
I'm begging you Lord, i've taking all I can take.
And seizures got me seizing, what's the reason I
shake?
As I wake, I am hoping to hear something good.
Send me a miracle that only YOU could.
Make this new cyst, not exist, if you would.
But if this is your plan, I understand..
UNDERSTOOD.
Tell me what's good. Tell me I'm fine.
When you bring me to my knees, in pain, is it a
sign?
4 different disorders I have in my spine,
feeling left in the rain in pain all the time.
Is there a reason or rhyme, Am I paying my dues?

Is my past coming up and it's under review?
I wish I knew why, I'd rewind and "undo",
All of my flaws, I would pause to "redo".
But this is what's true.
All of our past mistakes, make up YOU.
Without our mistakes we wouldn't have a BREAKTHROUGH.
No lessons to learn, that turned you BRAND NEW.
But what did I do to deserve this distress?
Did I bring it on myself because my life was a mess?
How do I remain in this pain I'm depressed.
My nerves are compressed and I'm confessing my stress.
The rest, I am leaving to you, in your hands.
Because God only you, could carry me through all this sand.
My feet they have failed me, but you took me by the hand,
Because you chose to then "BREAK ME", to Make ME, UNDERSTAND.
You're GRAND, and I know that you don't make mistakes.
Maybe my seizures, are to shake me awake.
Maybe your message I need not to forsake.
Open my eyes, and realize what's at stake.
You BREAK ME, to MAKE ME, not skip a beat.
And maybe there's reason you've crippled my feet.
You want me to walk, one day, down YOUR street.
Streets made of gold, where I'm told we shall meet.
How sweet it will be to meet you in time.
So maybe there's a reason you've crippled my spine.

Maybe you broke me, to rebuild me, re-align.
REDO ME, a NEW ME, be truly REFINED.
Send me a sign that maybe I'm right,
and all of these surgeries are worth every fight.
There's too many to come, but I'll pray every night.
And trust in God's plan, and hold his hand, oh so
TIGHT.

"Crazed"

These thoughts in my head are steady racing.
I'm wearing the floor thin from all this pacing.
My brain won't relax, it needs a vacation.
It's angry and hostile, I'm scared what I'm facing.
What do you do when your heads in a haze,
And you're all confused and feeling crazed.
When you're scared of yourself and won't be amazed,
if you beat yourself up again, in a bipolar rage.
How can you stop yourself from feeling so mad,
when you can't even explain the feelings you had?
And how can you tell yourself that things aren't so bad.
When you're back in a slump and feeling so sad.
I wish I could explain the thoughts in my head.
But I feel disconnected from my body instead.
I feel like I'm dreaming, or asleep in my bed,
And my mind is a nightmare, that I often dread.
There's this voice in my head, and it's daring me to die.
Tells me to kill myself, and it wants me to try.
A psychotic episode, my doctors are calling it by.
And thinking these meds will help me get by.
I'm battling demons that mess with my head.
They want me to take my own life instead,
of living for Jesus, they want me dead.
They want to control my soul I dread.
But I'll be damned, if I let them win.
Jesus I'm begging you don't let them in.
Stop all the demons before they begin.
And protect me with your blood, from this deadly sin.

I'm living for you, not dying for them, Lord.
I have your protection, like a shield and the sword.
When I hear their voices I seek help, rest assured.
I check myself in at 3 South, psych ward.
I refuse to let my loved ones find me dead.
Out of my mind, covered in blood I shed,
I'd rather fight back against the demons instead,
by seeking professional help and the blood JESUS shed.
I want to help others what to do in this case.
When the demons won't stop and they're up in your face.
Shout out God's name, and spray it like mace.
Blinding your demons, back to hell to their place.
Get on your knees and pray them away.
But still listen to advice that your doctors say.
It could take an army, with God leading the way.
But don't hesitate to ever seek help right away.
We are all battling Demons, of many kinds.
Some of them physically, some in our minds.
But the answer is Jesus, and he's easy to find.
Just say a prayer, because he's there, ALL the time.

"End of your rope"

We sometimes get so stressed, that we give up hope.
We are down on our luck, at the end of our rope.
So we start to complain, pass blame, and mope.
And forget all our faith, when we need it to cope.
How do we expect to get through all the stress,
if we don't give it to Jesus, to decompress?
We should give him our worries, our thanks, and confess,
Our sins and convictions and believe we'll be blessed.
And we can't be ungrateful when we don't get our way.
We can't lose our faith and walk away.
We must always BELIEVE, be HOPEFUL and PRAY.
And thank God for the lessons he taught us that day.
Because we need him the most, when we're at our worst.
We can't turn our backs and go in reverse.
When we struggle the most, always put GOD first.
Because he'll carry us through sand, to quench our thirst.
And when we are broken and falling apart,
God picks up the pieces to our Broken Heart.
He mends them together, a brand new start.
And restores our faith, scoring off of the chart.
So remember when you're stressing at the end of your rope.
To never give up and start to mope.
Because Jesus will cleanse your soul like soap.
And wash away worries, so never lose HOPE.

"Too Blessed to be stressed"

I'm too blessed to be stressed,
in this world that's a mess.
This world's in distress, and each day is a test.
We push through the rest,
And come out still our best.
And confess that our FAITH is what stood the true test.
Or did we moan, did we cry?
Did we wine and deny, The man in the sky?
Quickly blame the BIG GUY.
When we don't get our way are we quick to defy?
Turn our backs to the sky, lose our faith , let it fly.
Let it go, let it soar, Let it float out the door.
All beliefs we've endured, we believe them no more.
"Poor me, how can it be, the LORD let me hit the floor."
So we pout and act unsure, of all he's done for us before.
Hit the floor, bow our heads.
We should be grateful but instead,
we can't see the blood he shed.
And ignore the words he's said.
Breaking bread, wasting food ,despite who's fed.

We're NOT worth the blood he bled , but STILL he'd do it all AGAIN.
So if we lost our way. He'll invite us back to pray.
He even loves the ones astray.
But wants us home where we can stay.
Let's repent. That's the way.
Ask forgiveness for all today.
And he'll forgive us where we lay,
So let's pray our sins away.

"Chasing dreams"

How many others can admit when you're wrong?
See, I'm wrong all the time and it's hard to stay strong.
I wish I could say I knew where I belong.
But the truth of the matter, I've been wrong all along.
I know what I want but it's hard to achieve,
when dreams that you're chasing are hard to believe.
I've often chose paths that caused me to grieve,
so how can I trust the next plans I conceive.
I can map out my life, and watch it unfold.
And pray that it matches up to expectations I hold.
Because the paths that i've chosen left me out in the cold.
And the "SECRET TO SUCCESS ", is still untold.
How can I find happiness when I only see pain?
And where is the shelter when I'm left in the rain?
How can I Drive when I can't see my lane?
I'm blinded to the success that I'm needing to gain.
How do I know which moves I should make?
And how do I know which steps to take?
When the road that I travel could be my biggest mistake.
Should I give it a try, hit the gas, or the brakes?
These are the times that I wish I could see,
the end of the road that's in front of me.
I could ask for directions, because advice is free.
But at the end of the day, it's all up to me.
I could be a journalist or a movie star.
Or I could stay where I'm at and not get far.
I could choose to stand still and stay at this bar,
Or chase down my dreams, climb into my car.

when opportunity knocks, will I let her come in?
Or fear the unknown, scared of change once again.
Am i so used to "LOSING", that i'm scared of a "WIN?"
And fear money and success could change me within.
What do i do at the end of the day?
Do I trust my own heart not to lead me astray?
Do I listen to others and what they will say?
Or put my faith in the only man that knows the way. Let me
pray!!

"Dear God"

DEAR GOD, send me someone that I can hold through all the cold.
Someone I can have to cherish,love, and hug me til I'm old.
DEAR GOD, send me someone I can trust that will uphold,
All the love I have to give, and give it back without it told.
DEAR GOD, find a man that I can follow that can lead me down that path.
Hold my hand and guide me blinded, lift me kindly on his raft.
DEAR GOD, send me someone who can be my better half.
Who can love me when I'm dirty, right before my bubble half.
DEAR GOD, I barely ask you for requests.
I appreciate the things you've done for me, I'm truly blessed.
DEAR GOD, I'm just lonely and deprèssed.
Please find me someone you would think would treat me best.
DEAR GOD, i beg you please on bended knee.
Send me someone who accepts me for the person that is me.

DEAR GOD, I'm so desperate in my plee.
Can you hear me just this once and let me live so happily.
DEAR GOD, this is the update that I'm sending.
Thank you for the blessings and I got my happy ending.
DEAR GOD, on my knees now I am bending,
Thank you for everything In life and for this heart that you are mending.
DEAR GOD... DEAR GOD...

"Dear Heavenly Father"

Dear Heavenly Father,
We give thanks to you each day we live,
For the beautiful blessings each day you give.
I wanted to thank you from the depths of my heart,
For reuniting this family, I feared grew apart.
You delivered my man from his fears and his sorrows,
And showed him the light that will brighten tomorrow.
And you're guiding my children with your beautiful voice.
Through their journey of righteousness to each coming choice.
And you've joined us as one, to preform as a team.
And I thank you dear Lord, for fulfilling this dream.
Now I'm bowing my head, on my knees I will pray.
For the miracle you've given us, in the past and today.
For the babies so tiny, that have grown to be well.
And for the man who has ran, whom you picked up when he fell.
And the children in the family in need of some love.
That you placed in the household of kisses and hugs.
And the survivors of Cancer or and disease,
Only you God could relieve them of their miseries.
And those you have guided to do right through their wrong.

And those who are weak, who you helped to be strong.
And those who are blind, you have given a vision.
And the ones who were deaf, heard your voice and have listened.
And all who were sick, who you've risen from bed.
And every mouth that was hungry that our dear Lord has fed.
And for each and every problem that you've helped to be solved,
We kneel before you now, and thank you God, you're involved.
God bless all the children, the moms, and the dads.
Watch over our families through good, and through bad.
So Heavenly father, I must now rest my head,
And put my faith in your hands, as i climb into bed.
Amen.

" I used to be"

I used to be wild and running the streets,
looking for trouble and mission complete.
Steal from the stores, even the shoes on my feet,
were not mine to take, I was lost in deceit.
I was lost in this world, I was too blind to see,
that any good in my life wasn't coming from me.
I was bitter, so spiteful, so hateful you see.
And obsessed with revenge if you did wrong to me.
I was so quick to hurt you and see you in pain,
if I felt you deserved it, I was evil and vain.
So quick to fight and act insane,
vandalizing property and wouldn't refrain.
I was bad to the core but thought I was good.
If I could change some things now, I definitely would.
I would've done better like I know that I should.
What I didn't knew then, is NOW understood.
I thought I was heading to Heaven one day,
but Satan was laughing and leading the way.
I was heading to Hell for his torture and play.
And didn't have a clue I'd be there for the stay. But
God is so good that he wanted me to see,
that this isn't the life that he wanted for me.
So he opened my eyes so he can finally see,
the person inside that he meant me to be.
I'm still not an Angel, even though it's my name.

But I'm no longer vengeful, spiteful or insane.
I learned to forgive, and wish no bad on their name.
Because God forgave me, so I WILL do the same.

"So Full of hate"

This world is so sick and so full of hate.
And friends are dividing over unfriendly debate.
We all have opinions, some might not be great.
But should we really lose friends just cause they can't relate.
Just wait, for a second. Step into their shoes,
And hear what they say before you choose.
We might not have facts and we might be confused.
But that isn't a reason, that friends we should lose.
I refuse, to be a part of what this is about.
Whether race or religion, or political pouts.
I see all the hatred as we all sit and shout,
and not one person's willing, to hear anyone else out.
I doubt they will listen to anything i write.
Because they're all so concerned with winning the fight.
Opinions are blinding each and everyone's sight,
That we'll put our friends down, just to prove we are right.
So tonight,i will choose to join in at my pace.
I'm here not to win, but to pleade my case.
No politics, religion, or the color of our face,
Should divide us, cuz we ALL, are of the HUMAN race.
So in case we all forgot, the blood we bleed is all the same.
And the Lord will not be happy that we call each other names.
We DON'T have to all agree, to just respect each other's game.

We can all have our opinions, without putting yours to shame.
So refrain, from getting angry when your friends feel how they do.
You can't change someone's opinion, of their strongest point of view.
I'm entitled to my own, and you're entitled to yours too.
Just remember to still love each other when debates are through.

www.ingramcontent.com/pod-product-compliance
Lightning Source LLC
Chambersburg PA
CBHW051744130826
49812CB00033B/996
* 9 7 8 9 3 5 7 4 4 0 3 7 0 *